Dear Friend,

I am pleased to send you this copy of *My Jesus Is . . . Everything* by my sister Anne Graham Lotz. Anne is the founder and president of AnGeL Ministries, as well as a respected author and evangelist.

In this powerful book, Anne presents scriptures, stories, and poetry that all point to the primary truth of the Bible: Jesus is everything. He is our Lord and Savior, "the way, the truth, and the life" (John 14:6). Jesus is the One who will guide us through life. He is our source for strength and courage in difficult times. He "is even at the right hand of God, [and] also makes intercession for us" (Romans 8:34). As you read this book, I pray that you will recognize and trust Jesus as your everything.

For more than sixty years, the Billy Graham Evangelistic Association has worked to take the Good News of Jesus Christ throughout the world by every effective means available, and I'm excited about what God will do in the years ahead.

We would appreciate knowing how our ministry has touched your life. May God richly bless you.

Sincerely,

Franklin Graham
President

To learn more about our ministry, please contact us:

IN THE U.S.:
Billy Graham Evangelistic Association
1 Billy Graham Parkway
Charlotte, NC 28201-0001
BillyGraham.org
info@bgea.org
Toll-free: 1-877-247-2426

IN CANADA:
Billy Graham Evangelistic
   Association of Canada
20 Hopewell Way NE
Calgary, AB T3J 5H5
BillyGraham.ca
Toll-free: 1-888-393-0003

MY JESUS IS ... *Everything*

Anne Graham Lotz

COUNTRYMAN®

A Division of Thomas Nelson Publishers

NASHVILLE DALLAS MEXICO CITY RIO DE JANEIRO

THOMAS NELSON
Since 1798

BILLY GRAHAM
Evangelistic Association

Always Good News.

Copyright © 2005, 2013 by Anne Graham Lotz

Published by J. Countryman®, a division of Thomas Nelson, Inc.,
Nashville, Tennessee 37214. Thomas Nelson, Inc., titles may be
purchased in bulk for educational, business, fund-raising, or sales
promotional use. For information, please e-mail SpecialMarkets@
ThomasNelson.com.

Published in association with the literary agency of Alive
Communications, Inc., 1465 Kelly Johnson Blvd., Suite 320, Colorado
Springs, CO 80920.

Unless otherwise noted, Scripture quotations are taken from THE
NEW KING JAMES VERSION. © 1982 by Thomas Nelson, Inc.
Used by permission. All rights reserved.

Scripture quotations marked NIV are taken from the Holy Bible, New
International Version®, NIV®. Copyright © 1973, 1978, 1984 by
Biblica, Inc.™ Used by permission of Zondervan. All rights reserved
worldwide. www.zondervan.com.

Designed by The DesignWorks Group, Robin Black,
www.thedesignworksgroup.com

ISBN-13: 978-1-4003-7538-7

Printed in the United States of America

13 14 15 16 17 BP 5 4 3 2 1

For God was pleased to have all his

fullness dwell in him.

Colossians 1:19 (niv)

Just Look at Jesus!

Do you want to know what is on the mind of God?

> Then look at Jesus!

Do you want to know the will of God?

> Then look at Jesus!

Do you want to know what is in the heart of God?

> Then look at Jesus!

Jesus is the exact revelation of what is

> on the mind

> and in the heart

> and in the will of God!

Who is Jesus?

What is there about Him that makes Him so
        compelling that
     . . . some of the greatest architectural achievements
        in Europe were built for worship of Him?
     . . . some of the world's most beautiful art was
        created to honor Him?
     . . . some of the world's most glorious music was
        written to praise Him?

In the beginning was the Word,
and the Word was with God and the Word was God. . . .
In Him was life, and the life was the light of men.
JOHN 1:1, 4

Jesus claimed to be the Son of God. He claimed to
be God walking the earth in a man's body! Do you
believe Him? Who do you say that He is?

The Son is the radiance
of God's glory and
the exact representation of
his being, sustaining all things
by his powerful word.
After he had provided
purification for sins, he sat
down at the right hand of the
Majesty in heaven.

HEBREWS 1:3 (NIV)

My Jesus

He is enduringly strong.

He is entirely sincere.

He is eternally steadfast.

He is immortally gracious.

He is imperially powerful.

He is impartially merciful.

He is the greatest phenomenon that has ever
       crossed the horizons of the globe.

He is God's Son.

He is the sinner's Savior.

He is the captive's Ransom.

He is the Breath of Life.

He is the centerpiece of civilization.

He stands in the solitude of Himself.

He is august and He is unique.

He is unparalleled and He is unprecedented.

He is undisputed and He is undefiled.

He is unsurpassed and He is unshakable.

He is the lofty idea in philosophy.

He is the highest personality in psychology.

He is the supreme subject in literature.

He is the unavoidable problem in higher criticism.

He is the fundamental doctrine of theology.

He is the Cornerstone, the Capstone,

      and the stumbling Stone of all religion.

He is the miracle of the ages.

My Jesus is . . . *Everything!*

He Is More

The Word who was in the beginning with God is a

living Person.

But He is more.

He is the living expression of what is on God's mind.

But He is more.

He is the living expression of what is on God's heart.

But He is even more.

He is the very heart of the Almighty God of the universe

laid bare for all to see!

They Knew Him

Adam knew Him as a beloved Father.

Eve knew Him as the original Homemaker.

Noah knew Him as the Refuge from the storm.

Abraham knew Him as a Friend.

Moses knew Him as the Redeemer.

Rahab knew Him as the gracious Savior.

David knew Him as his Shepherd.

Elijah knew Him as the Almighty.

Daniel knew Him as the Lion Tamer.

Mary Magdalene knew Him as the Bondage Breaker.

Martha knew Him as the Promise Keeper.

Lazarus knew Him as the Resurrection and the Life.

Bartimaeus knew Him as the Light of the World.

John knew Him as the glorious King upon the throne.

Surely you and I can know Him too!

About twenty-five years ago, without a crisis experience but with an unexplainable, intense yearning, I made the decision to seek to know God. Personally. Intimately. Accurately. Experientially. I decided that if each of these Bible characters could know Him, then I could too.

If God hasn't changed, if He is enduringly the same, then if they knew Him and I didn't, the fault must lie with me. So I began a pilgrimage to know God, and that pilgrimage continues to this day. I don't know Him today as well as I want to or should, but I know Him better today than I did twenty-five years ago. I know Him better today than I did one year ago.

*Knowing Jesus is my joy
and reason for living.*

He is . . .

    the Wind beneath my wings,

    the Treasure I seek,

    the Foundation on which I build,

    the Song in my heart,

    the Object of my desire,

    the Breath of my life—

    He is my All in all!

The Master Builder

Years ago a man was driving his car down the road when the engine sputtered and stalled. Try as he might, the driver could not restart the engine. As he stood glaring at it, a polished black limo pulled up beside him. The chauffeur hastily jumped out and opened the back door for an elegantly dressed gentleman. The man asked the driver about his problem and offered to take a look under the hood. The man scoffed at the idea of such a finely dressed man having any knowledge of mechanics, but no one else had stopped to help, so he accepted the assistance and threw open the hood.

The gentleman leaned over the engine, twisted a few wires, tapped a few cables, and tightened a few plugs. Then he told the driver to try to start the car. This time the car responded immediately.

As he closed the hood, the driver thanked the gentleman profusely. Then he asked for his name.

The gentleman replied simply, "Henry Ford."

Henry Ford had made the car, so he had known exactly what was wrong with it and how to fix it! Jesus Christ is the One by Whom, for Whom, and through Whom everything was made. He knows what's wrong in your life and how to fix it.

Does your life need mending? Who or what do you know that needs "fixing"? Jesus, as the creator of life, knows how to make it work. Let Him take charge. Give Him the authority to put it right.

The Lord is near to those who have a broken heart,
and saves such as have a contrite spirit.
Many are the afflictions of the righteous,
but the Lord delivers him out of them all.

PSALM 34:18–19

Anne Graham Lotz

Jesus Makes Change Possible

Therefore, if anyone is in Christ, he is a new creation;
old things have passed away;
behold, all things have become new.

2 CORINTHIANS 5:17

MY JESUS IS . . . *Everything*

My Jesus

No means of measure can define His limitless love . . .
No far-seeing telescope can bring into visibility the
        coastline of His shoreless supply . . .
No barrier can hinder Him from pouring out His
        blessings . . .

He forgives and He forgets.
    He creates and He cleanses.
        He restores and He rebuilds.
            He heals and He helps.
                He reconciles and He redeems.
                    He comforts and He carries.
                        He lifts and He loves.

            He is the God of the second chance,
                    the fat chance,
                        the slim chance,
                            the no chance.

My Jesus is . . . *Everything!*

Knowing God

is more than just being saved or being born again,
just as knowing my husband is more than just saying
marriage vows at the wedding altar. Knowing God
involves an intimate, personal relationship that is
developed over time through prayer and getting
answers to prayer, through Bible study and applying
its teaching to our lives, through obedience and
experiencing the power of God, through moment-
by-moment submission to Him that results in a
moment-by-moment filling of the Holy Spirit.

God gives me peace and joy within as I put
myself in His hands, trusting Him to infuse my life
with His love.

Born of the Spirit

Just as the virgin Mary conceived the physical life of the Son of God, you and I conceive the spiritual life of the Son of God when we are "born again." From that moment on, we are essentially two people on the inside. We have the mind, emotions, and will that we were physically born with, but we now also have the mind, emotions, and will of Christ within us. We have a spiritual "implant" of the life of Jesus Christ within our bodies. This is actually Jesus in the Person of the Holy Spirit.

This "implanting" of the life of Christ is a supernatural miracle. It is something God does in response to our humble confession and sincere repentance of sin coupled with our deliberate, personal faith in His Son because of His death on the cross as our atoning sacrifice and His resurrection.

The Question

Nicodemus said to Him,
"How can a man be born when he is old?
Can he enter a second time
into his mother's womb and be born?"
Jesus answered, "Most assuredly, I say to you,
unless one is born of water and the Spirit,
he cannot enter the kingdom of God.
That which is born of the flesh is flesh, and that
which is born of the Spirit is spirit.
Do not marvel that I said to you,
'You must be born again.'"

JOHN 3:4–7

MY JESUS IS . . . *Everything*

Jesus' appeal to Nicodemus to believe and be born again in order to receive eternal life and be assured of a place in heaven is God's Gospel in a nutshell. What a wonder it must have been to have heard for the first time, "For God so loved the world that He gave His only begotten Son, that whoever believes in Him should not perish but have everlasting life" (John 3:16)—from the mouth of God Himself!

Thousands of men and women throughout the ages have experienced the life-changing impact of the words Nicodemus had the privilege of hearing first. It's hard to imagine how stunning Jesus' words must have been to a man who heard them with an Old Testament perspective. Even now, two thousand years later, we marvel at the beautiful way God has provided what we need most.

Being
born again
is God's solution
to our need
for love
and life
and light . . .
and a fresh start.

Our World is looking for love. As human beings, we need to love and be loved. But we're looking in all the wrong places.

We look for it
    from a parent,
        from a child,
            from a sibling,
                from a spouse,
                    from a lover,
                        from a friend,
                      from a pet.

But our parents grow old and die,
    our children grow up and live their own lives,
      our siblings move out and on,
        our spouses are too busy or too tired,
          our lovers become jealous or bored,
        our friends are superficial
      or selfish,
    our pets can't speak or counsel.

Who can truly *understand* the need of the human heart?
Who can meet the *need* of our hearts?

Where is love found?

Jesus revealed to Nicodemus the profound insight that

love is found
in the heart of God.

Man was created by God to know and love Him in a permanent, personal relationship. The eternal plan to reconcile man with God, to forgive him of all sins, originated in the heart of God. It was motivated by His great love.

For God so loved you that He gave His Son, His only Son, the Son Whom He loved—He gave heaven's most precious Treasure—He gave everything He had in order to offer you eternal life.

We love Him because He first loved us.

1 JOHN 4:19

One thing we can know for sure is that God loves you and me. How do we know that?

We know it by just looking at the cross where He proved His love for the world that mocks Him and ignores Him and despises Him and scorns Him and rejects Him.

We look at the cross and see "I love you" written in red.

"Come to Me,

all you who labor and are heavy laden,
and I will give you rest. Take My yoke upon you
and learn from Me, for I am gentle and lowly in heart,
and you will find rest for your souls.
For My yoke is easy and My burden is light."

MATTHEW 11:28–30

God's appeal to come is
striking in its simplicity,
stunning in its clarity,
supreme in its authority,
solemn in its inescapability,
strong in its necessity,
satisfying in its complexity,
sufficient in its centrality,
successful in its sufficiency.

An archbishop of a certain country was invited to Chicago to give a lecture in a theological school. While sightseeing aboard a city bus, he felt a finger tap him on the shoulder. He turned to look into the ebony face of an obviously poor woman seated behind him. She asked, "Mister, has you ever been born again?" The archbishop replied with dignity, "My dear madam, I am the archbishop of my church. I am here to give a lecture at the theological seminary."

As the bus rolled to a stop, the woman looked at the proud, religious man and persisted bluntly, "Mister, that ain't what I asked you. I asked you, 'Has you been born again?'" Then she walked off the bus and out of his life.

But her words burned in his soul. He located a Gideon Bible in his hotel room and opened it to read the story of Nicodemus. He knew that even with all of his religious training he had never been born again. So he slipped to his knees right there and God answered his heart's cry to just give him Jesus.

A Wedding Miracle

 When the shortage of wine first became known at the wedding feast in Cana, it seemed on the surface that Jesus would do nothing. But Mary knew Him well enough to know that He would act in His own time and in His own way. Her expectancy must have infected the servants who continued to wait quietly for His instructions. Jesus issued a command that seemed to have nothing to do with the shortage of wine: "Fill the jars with water." Then he told them, "Now draw some out and take it to the master of the banquet." They must have held their breath as the master lifted it to his lips and "tasted the water that had been turned into wine" and declared it "the best" (John 2:7–10 NIV).

It was such a quiet miracle. Nothing flashy that would have drawn attention to Jesus. Just a quiet change that saved a young bridegroom's honor and answered a mother's prayer.

Is that what you desperately want?

Just a quiet miracle in your marriage or your home or even your ministry that would turn the water into wine? Then invite Jesus to come in, inform Him of the problem, and invest Him with full authority. Jesus makes change possible even when the love has run out of your marriage. He invites you to taste and enjoy the "new wine" as from your heart you thank God for just giving you Jesus!

For with God
nothing will be impossible.

LUKE 1:37

My Jesus

He discharges the debtors.

He delivers the captives.

He defends the feeble.

He blesses the young.

He serves the unfortunate.

He regards the aged.

He rewards the diligent.

He beautifies the meek.

He is the key to knowledge.

He is the wellspring of wisdom.

He is the foundation of faith.

He is the doorway of deliverance.

He is the pathway to peace.

He is the roadway of righteousness.

He is the gateway to glory.

He is the highway to happiness.

My Jesus is . . . *Everything!*

Today Jesus still waits beside the well of water to meet with those who will come to Him

—just as He waited by the well in Samaria to meet one outcast woman who had all the symptoms of emptiness and unhappiness. There was only one reason "He needed to go through Samaria" (John 4:4). He had a divine appointment. Have you ever considered that you have a divine appointment when you get up early for your quiet time of prayer and meditation on His Word? . . . That Jesus is patiently, personally waiting to meet with you there?

What a difference it would make in our attitude of expectancy and our habit of consistency if we truly wrapped our hearts around the knowledge that Jesus Himself is waiting to meet with us.

Jesus knows

the small secrets of your heart,

the unspoken dreams of your imagination,

the unrevealed thoughts of your mind,

the emotional shards of your feelings,

the paralyzing fears for your future,

the bitter resentments of your past,

the joys and heartaches,

the pleasures and pain,

the successes and failures,

the honors and humiliations,

the deeds and the doubts.

*He knows all about you,
inside and out,
past, present, and future.*

Anne Graham Lotz

The Woman Running on Empty

The Samaritan woman was dissatisfied spiritually and emotionally. It was customary for the women during that era to come to the well in groups early in the morning or early in the evening. It was the equivalent of standing a few extra minutes at the water cooler in the office to pass the time of day with a coworker or talking over a backyard fence. It was simply a time to satisfy the emotional needs for friendship and companionship. Yet this woman had come in the middle of the day. Alone. Why? The obvious reason is that she was a social outcast. The Samaritan woman had no one to confide in,

no one to open her heart to,

no one to relax with,

no one to share with,

no one to laugh with,

no one to cry with.

MY JESUS IS . . . *Everything*

Praise God for the blood of Jesus that is sufficient to cover all of our sins! All of them—

past sins,
    present sins,
        future sins,
            big sins,
                small sins,
                    or medium-size sins—
                        it makes no difference.

They are all under the blood of Jesus, and we are free just to enjoy our forgiveness!

Other Wells

Jesus knew the woman at the well had searched for satisfaction and had come up short. He knew her heart was empty, without love or self-worth or meaning or fulfillment or happiness. And so He gently but pointedly replied, "Whoever drinks of this water will thirst again" (John 4:13). What was "this water"? The woman took it to mean the water in Jacob's well, but Jesus was speaking to her heart. All those who look to draw their satisfaction from the wells of the world— pleasure, popularity, position, possessions, politics, power, prestige, finances, family, friends, fame, fortune, career, children, church, clubs, sports, sex, success, recognition, reputation, religion, education, entertainment, exercise, honors, health, hobbies—will soon be thirsty again!

If you look for deep, lasting satisfaction from any of these wells the world offers, you're wasting your time.

MY JESUS IS . . . *Everything*

While the world's wells can be meaningful and pleasing temporarily, they eventually leave the seeker emptier than before, wondering,

"Is that all there is?"

"LORD, THOU HAST MADE ME FOR THYSELF.
THEREFORE MY HEART IS RESTLESS TILL IT
FINDS ITS REST IN THEE."

ST. AUGUSTINE

"Each of us has a
God-shaped hole in our hearts
that only a personal relationship
with God can fill."

Viktor Frankl

*"A time is coming and
has now come
when the true worshipers will
worship the Father in spirit
and truth, for they are
the kind of worshipers
the Father seeks.
God is spirit,
and his worshipers
must worship in spirit
and in truth."*

JOHN 4:23–24 (NIV)

How many blessings from God have you and I missed because we didn't like the packaging? Are we allowing prejudices to deafen our ears and blind our eyes because the speaker is of . . .

another gender

or race

or culture

or denomination

or economic level

or educational background?

Because the messenger . . .

has a different color skin

or speaks with a different accent

or wears funny-looking clothes

or worships with contemporary choruses

or appears in unexpected places—

have we thrown up an invisible barrier?

While the woman of Samaria and I have many differences, we have one thing in common. I, too, find myself from time to time running on empty.

In the busyness of ministry,
   the pressures of responsibility,
     the demands of family,
       the weariness of activity,
         the excitement of opportunity,
I sometimes wake up and realize,

"I am so dry and thirsty."

My Jesus

He supplies strength to the weary.
   He increases power to the faint.
      He offers escape to the tempted.

He sympathizes with the hurting.
   He saves the hopeless.
      He shields the helpless.
         He sustains the homeless.

He gives purpose to the aimless.
   He gives reason to the meaningless.
      He gives fulfillment to our emptiness.
         He gives light in the darkness.
            He gives comfort in our loneliness.
               He gives fruit in our barrenness.
                  He gives heaven to the hopeless.
                     He gives life to the lifeless!

My Jesus is . . . *Everything!*

Come Away

What pressure have you recently been under? Do you feel emotionally drained, physically exhausted, and spiritually depleted as well? Jesus sees and understands your needs.

Jesus saw the physical, emotional, and spiritual needs of His friends and knew the solution was a time of quiet rest and reflection. And He knows the solution is the same for you and me today. So He invites us, as He did His disciples, "Come with Me by yourself to a quiet place and get some rest."

Often when I am under stress and pressure, I feel one of my greatest needs is to get a good night's sleep. But I've found that physical rest alone is not enough to revive my flagging spirit. I need the spiritual revival that comes from spending quiet time alone with Jesus in prayer and in thoughtful meditation on His Word.

Show me Your ways, O Lord;

Teach me Your paths.
Lead me in Your truth and teach me,
For You are the God of my salvation;
On You I wait all the day.
Remember, O Lord, Your tender mercies
and Your lovingkindnesses . . .
According to your mercy remember me.

Psalm 25:4–7

my jesus is . . . *Everything*

A careful study of the life of Jesus reveals that as pressed as He was, He "often withdrew to lonely places and prayed" (Luke 5:16 NIV). If Jesus felt He needed time alone in prayer with His Father, why do you and I think we can get by without it?

Again and again, I have been amazed to discover that the verse of Scripture or thought or insight that God seems to give me in my early morning quiet time with Him is the very same verse or insight or thought I am called on to give to someone else during the day. Many times I have wondered how I would have been able to speak a "word that sustains the weary" (Isaiah 50:4 NIV) had I not first received it for myself in those brief, early morning retreats. Jesus offers us ample resources, but we have to receive them from Him in order to impart them to others.

Draw near to God
and He will draw near to you.

JAMES 4:8

Do you think Jesus only cares about things like heaven and hell?

About things like forgiveness and sin or holiness and wickedness? Jesus does care about those things. But He also cares about your job, about whether your child makes the sports team, about your children's college tuition, and about the roof that leaks and the cranky transmission in your car. Jesus cares even if the problem we face is largely of our own making. Jesus cares about your physical needs today, just as He cared for those of the hungry crowd so long ago. The people who had tagged along "to the far shore of the Sea of Galilee" (John 6:1 NIV), interrupting Jesus' retreat, were people who had first sought to be with Jesus Himself. There was no dire emergency. Everyone would have survived going without one meal. They hadn't been invited, and when they had barged in on someone else's vacation, they had overstayed without planning ahead. But Jesus cared. The people weren't just given a snack or a bite to tide them over until they could get a full meal, they "all had enough to eat" (John 6:12 NIV).

Recipe for a Miracle

 How had Jesus accomplished the miracle of the feeding of five thousand with five loaves and two fish? The formula is really quite simple.

> The disciples gave it all.
> Jesus took it all.
> God blessed it all.
> Jesus broke it all.
> Jesus supplied it all.
> The disciples gave it all.
> The entire multitude was fed!

This simple formula is one that I have followed continuously for the past twenty-five years, especially in ministry. I have given Jesus all that I am, as well as all that I have, which isn't much. I am a housewife who does my family's grocery shopping, cooking, cleaning, and laundry. I have very limited education and no formal seminary training or Bible schooling. I have a shy, timid personality that tends to be painfully self-conscious. So when I say I have given all to Jesus, I assure you that I make the original five loaves and two fish look plentiful indeed! What I do have is an intense longing to know God, and that longing has given me an insatiable desire to know His Word—for myself.

And my God will meet all your needs
according to his glorious riches in Christ Jesus.
PHILIPPIANS 4:19 (NIV)

 When I gave it all to Jesus, He accepted it! He has acknowledged that I am not enough in myself to meet anyone else's need. Yet He has blessed what I have given Him, broken and rearranged it to suit Himself until I knew my resources were even more inadequate than I had thought, and He has given me insights into Him and His Word that only He could give.

MY JESUS IS . . . *Everything*

Who is your multitude?

Who are the people God wants you to help
Him feed? Who are the people you come
into contact with who are hungry for the
bread of God's Word? And what are your "loaves and
fish"? What very limited and inadequate resources do
you have? Wouldn't you like to experience the thrill
of participating with Him in the miracle of feeding
others with what you have received from Him—and
finding that it's enough to satisfy their hunger?

If all you ever attempt is that which
you know you can do or have the resources for,
how will you ever discover what He can do?

There are times when I have gotten the distinct impression from some Christians that the Holy Spirit is an optional extra, reserved primarily for benedictions, baptisms, and those we label "charismatics." Others give the impression that He is more like a heavenly genie in a bottle, Who, if you rub Him with the right mixture of prayer and faith, will perform miracles for you.

But the Holy Spirit is not an optional extra!

He is not to be reserved only for special occasions or exclusive groups, nor is He a trick-performing genie. He is a divine necessity Who is imparted to each and every believer at the moment of conversion.

The Amplified Bible gives seven names that could be equally translated from the word for "Counselor." Each name, as defined by *Webster's Dictionary*, describes a different aspect of the Person of the Holy Spirit. He is our

COUNSELOR: One Whose profession is to give advice and manage causes.

COMFORTER: One Who relieves another of mental distress.

HELPER: One Who furnishes with relief or support; One Who is of use and who waits upon another.

INTERCESSOR: One Who acts between parties to reconcile differences.

ADVOCATE: One Who pleads the cause of another.

STRENGTHENER: One Who causes another to grow, become stronger, endure, and resist attacks.

STANDBY: One who can be relied upon either for regular use or in emergencies.

Wonderful Counselor

 Can you imagine how wonderful it would be to have Someone with these attributes in your life?

Are you distressed today? Then you need the Comforter.

Are you facing a major decision? Then you need the Counselor.

Do you need relief from, or support in, your responsibilities? Then you need the Helper.

Do you have a broken relationship? Then you need the Intercessor.

Are you being criticized, falsely accused, misunderstood? Then you need the Advocate.

Are you constantly defeated by habits of sin? Then you need the Strengthener.

Are you unprepared for an emergency? Then you need the Standby.

The Holy Spirit is everything that Jesus is!

Where is the Holy Spirit?

In the Garden of Eden, God had been with man.
In the Old Testament, God had appeared to man.
In the Tabernacle, God had dwelt among men.
In the history of Israel, God had spoken through man.
In the Gospels, God was visible as Man.
But at Pentecost, God became available to dwell in man!

 Since Pentecost two thousand years ago, the Holy Spirit has been available to anyone and everyone in the whole world! But He is a gentleman! He only comes into, or indwells, the person who deliberately—consciously—specifically—humbly—individually—personally invites Him.

My Jesus

He guards the young.
He seeks the stray.
He finds the lost.
He guides the faithful.
He rights the wronged.
He avenges the abused.
He defends the weak.
He comforts the oppressed.
He welcomes the prodigal.
He heals the sick.
He cleanses the dirty.

He beautifies the barren.
He restores the failure.
He mends the broken.
He blesses the poor.
He fills the empty.
He clothes the naked.
He satisfies the hungry.
He elevates the humble.
He forgives the sinner.
He raises the dead!

My Jesus is . . .
Everything!

Anne Graham Lotz

Why?

Why would a good God allow bad things to happen to good people? The problem of pain and questions about suffering are as old as the human race. But they remain the clinical subject of philosophical theories and intellectual sparring and theological debate until they become personal, until it's our homes or our children or our loved ones who are hurting. Then we simply have desperate questions that need direct answers.

> *The LORD is close to the brokenhearted*
> *and saves those who are crushed in spirit.*
>
> PSALM 34:18 (NIV)

As Jesus passed by,

He saw a man who was blind from birth.
And His disciples asked Him, saying,
"Rabbi, who sinned, this man or his parents,
that he was born blind?" Jesus answered,
"Neither this man nor his parents sinned, but that
the works of God should be revealed in him."

JOHN 9:1–3

 I wonder how many opportunities to meet
the needs of others God has given me when
I was

too self-absorbed,
   too self-centered,
      too self-conscious,
         too self-defensive,
            too self-pitying,
               too self-protecting
                  to notice.

Who would be helped, who would have his or her
needs met, if we just opened our eyes and really saw
those around us?

Is suffering due to God's punishment for sin?

The Bible clearly teaches that God's punishment for the guilt of sin is not suffering, but death. Sin is so serious in God's sight that even one sin calls for the death of the sinner. There is no amount of suffering that can obtain for us forgiveness of sin and rid us of guilt in God's sight. But Jesus stepped in and took God's punishment for our sins at the cross. When we claim His death for our sins, we are absolved of guilt.

He has forgiven our sins through the blood He shed at Calvary.

All suffering

is indirectly related to Adam and Eve's original sin at the beginning of human history. But suffering can also be the direct result of our own personal sins. I struggle with the pain of ulcers because of my sin of worry and lack of trust in the Lord. Migraine headaches and psychological stress can be caused by the sin of bitterness, anger, or the refusal to forgive someone who has wronged us. We can suffer injury in a car accident as the result of disobeying the authority of the traffic laws. We can suffer through the pain of divorce because we have refused to live by God's marriage principles.

When we suffer, it's a legitimate response to examine ourselves before God to determine if we are indeed suffering because of personal sin. If you are suffering today, the Bible says to confess your sins to the Lord, pray for release, and ask others to pray for your healing.

God's Opportunity

What physical, social, emotional, intellectual, or mental limitation do you have? Instead of blaming it on your doctor or parent or spouse or sibling or teacher or neighbor or boss or pastor or child . . . instead of seeing your handicap as someone's fault or even as an accident, consider that it might be an opportunity for God to display Himself through your life to others.

Paul said, "I will boast all the more gladly about my weaknesses, so that Christ's power may rest on me. That is why, for Christ's sake, I delight in weaknesses, in insults, in hardships, in persecutions, in difficulties. For when I am weak, then I am strong" (2 Corinthians 12:9–10 NIV).

God's grace and power
seem to reach their peak
when we are at our weakest point.

What kinds of trials have caused you to suffer grief?

 Could it be God has given you a platform of suffering from which you can be a witness of His power and grace to those who are watching? Because if we always feel good

and look good

and lead a good life;

if our kids always behave

and our boss is always pleased

and our home is always orderly

and our friends are always available

and our bank account is always sufficient

and our car always starts

and our bodies always feel good

and we are patient and kind and thoughtful and happy and loving, others shrug because they're capable of being that way too.

On the other hand, if

we have a splitting headache,
the kids are screaming,
the phone is ringing,
the boss is yelling,
the supper is burning,
yet we are still patient, kind, thoughtful,
happy, and loving,
the world sits up and takes notice.
The world knows that kind of behavior
is not natural.

It's supernatural.

MY JESUS IS . . . *Everything*

Looking back

over a difficult period, my thoughtful, confident
conclusion is that these storms of suffering have
increased and intensified in my life because Jesus
wanted me to soar higher in my relationship with
Him—

to fall deeper in love with Him,
to grow stronger in my faith in Him,
to be more consistent in my walk with Him,
to bear more fruit in my service to Him,
to draw closer to His heart,
to keep my focus on His face,
to live for His glory alone!

Growth in depth and strength and consistency and fruitfulness and ultimately in Christlikeness is only possible when the winds of life are contrary to personal comfort. Just as storms make it possible for eagles to soar, so suffering makes it possible for you and me to attain the highest pinnacles in the Christian life. Suffering develops our faith.

God uses it to accomplish His will, which can go against human logic and common sense. The reason for this is to focus on our faith, not on our friends . . . or ability . . . or resources . . . or knowledge . . . or strength . . . or *anything* other than Him alone.

MY JESUS IS . . . *Everything*

Just as a diamond

seems to sparkle more brilliantly when displayed in a black velvet case, so the radiant beauty of Christlike character seems to shine more splendidly against the backdrop of suffering. Even in Martha's grief over the death of Lazarus, the jewel of hope that seemed to have been birthed in her spirit sparkled. She eagerly went to Mary, drawing her aside privately to tell her, "The Teacher is here . . . and is asking for you" (John 11:28 NIV).

Are you desperate for your "Lazarus"? Where is your focus? If you are suffering, is your focus on the pain? Or the problems the pain produces? Or people who don't seem to understand or help as you think they should? Are you desperate enough to place your faith in Jesus alone? Sometimes He allows us to suffer so that we become a display case for His glory.

My Jesus

His office is manifold,
    and His promise is sure.
His life is matchless,
    and His goodness is limitless.
His mercy is enough,
    and His grace is sufficient.
His reign is righteous, His yoke is easy,
    and His burden is light.

He is indestructible. He is indescribable.
He is incomprehensible. He is inescapable.
He is invincible. He is irresistible. He is irrefutable.

I can't get Him out of my mind . . .
    And I can't get Him out of my heart.
I can't outlive Him . . .
    And I can't live without Him.

The Pharisees couldn't stand Him
  but found they couldn't stop Him.
Satan tried to tempt Him
  but found he couldn't trip Him.
Pilot examined Him on trial
  but found he couldn't fault Him.
The Romans crucified Him
  but found they couldn't take His life.
Death couldn't handle Him,

*and the grave couldn't
hold Him.*

My Jesus is . . . *Everything!*

Judas

was one of Jesus' very closest friends. He had been handpicked to be a disciple. Jesus had lovingly bathed his feet during the Last Supper in the upper room. But he betrayed his Lord and Friend with a kiss!

Although Jesus clearly knew the betrayal was coming, it was still a knife-like stab to His heart.

If only Judas had flung himself instead of the silver at the feet of Jesus and cried, "Jesus, I'm sorry. I don't know what got into me. I can't believe what I have done to You. I have betrayed You. Please forgive me."

Then Jesus would have forgiven Judas!

The entire detachment of soldiers, Roman officials, religious leaders, and Judas, who "was standing there with them" (John 18:6 NIV), fell flat on their faces before Him!

The Bible says that one day, "at the name of Jesus every knee should bow, in heaven and on earth and under the earth, and every tongue confess that Jesus Christ is Lord, to the glory of God the Father" (Philippians 2:10–11 NIV). Whether we want to or not, one day we will all bow before God's only Son.

Who do you know who has set him- or herself against Christ?

> A school administrator?
> A business employer?
> A secular corporation?
> A religious institution?
> A political agenda?
> A government policy?
> An entire culture?

Whoever, or whatever, sets themselves against Christ will find themselves sooner or later on their faces before Him!

They bound the hands of the Son of God!
The hands of the Creator!

Hands that had lifted in authority and calmed the
    storm at sea.
Hands that had gathered little children on His knee.
Hands that had smeared mud on the blind beggar's
    eyes and given him sight.
Hands that had touched the leper and cleansed him.
Hands that had broken the fish and the bread and fed
    five thousand people.
Hands that had hung the worlds in space.
Hands that had formed Adam from the dust of the
    ground.
Hands that had formed the very men who were now
    binding Him.

Have you ever felt bound . . .

   in a marriage where the love has run out?

    in a small home with small children?

     in a physical body wracked with pain?

      to an elderly parent with Alzheimer's?

       by responsibility that isn't really yours?

       to a job?

        by habits of sin?

        by memories of abuse?

Are you struggling with your bindings? Do you find that the more you fight against them, the more pain you inflict on yourself, so that you are miserable in your confinement? Sometimes binding is in the will of God.

As Jesus went through six trials, accused of blasphemy, tax evasion, and insurrection, where were His defenders?

Where was the paralyzed man who had lain beside the pool of Bethesda for thirty-eight years before Jesus healed him?

Where were the lepers He had cleansed?

Where was the adulterous woman He had saved from stoning and then instructed to sin no more?

Where was the Roman centurion whose servant had been healed at a great distance by the simple word of Jesus?

Where was the woman whose life's blood had seeped from her for twelve years who had been healed by simply touching the hem of His garment?

Where was the nobleman whose daughter arose from death when Jesus took her by the hand?

Where were the mute whose tongues had been loosed at the command of Jesus?

Where was the man who had been born blind to whom Jesus had given sight?

Where were Mary and Martha and Lazarus?

Where were the men and women and children whose lives Jesus had changed?

Where are they still?

As God's Son, God's only Son, the Son He loved, hung on the cross, the knife of God's fierce wrath against sin was lifted, and there was no one to stay the Father's hand. Instead, "He . . . did not spare his own Son, but gave him up for us all" (Romans 8:32 NIV). Jesus was God's Lamb and our Substitute Who endured the full force of God's wrath for your sins and mine when He was bound on the altar in our place.

In His tender, thoughtful care for His mother, Jesus, as He was dying, gives you and me a powerful lesson in how to overcome emotional suffering. Most of us increase our pain by dwelling on it or by analyzing it. We throw a pity party and expect others to join us. We spiral downward into depression, withdrawing into self-preoccupation.

But the way to overcome is not to focus on ourselves or on the pain, but to focus on the needs of others.

Only God in Christ has the power to forgive sin.

But you and I must confess it to Him personally, specifically, and honestly if we want to receive forgiveness. That word *confess* means to call sin by the same name that God does, to agree with God about your sin. When you do, God's Word promises,

> *"If we confess our sins,*
> *He is faithful and just to forgive us our sins and to*
> *cleanse us from all unrighteousness."*

1 JOHN 1:9

The blood of the Lamb that was shed on the altar of the cross ran down its wooden beam, down a hill called Calvary, and down through the years until it reaches us, where it has become a river that is deep enough to wash away all sin. Even if we have betrayed those we love most, as Judas did, we will be forgiven. That is what Jesus came to do. That is what He still comes to do.

If you agree,

pray this simple prayer by faith:

Dear God,

I choose to grasp the Lamb with my hands of faith and confess to You the hardness of my heart, the meanness of my thoughts, the coldness of my spirit, and the sinfulness of my life. I'm so sorry. I know it was for me—and because of me—that Jesus died. Please forgive me of all of my sins—big sins, medium sins, and small sins; past sins, present sins, and future sins. I want to exchange my filthy garments of sin for His spotless robe of righteousness.

Thank You for the cleansing fountain of the blood of Jesus that washes me white as snow. I know even now that I am clean and forgiven and "dressed" for heaven.

Thank You! Thank You! Thank You for just giving me Jesus!

In Christ Jesus, you are a new creation. Your sins are forgiven. Your guilt is atoned for. Your past is removed. Your future is secured. You have peace in your heart. You have purpose to your step. You are right with God.

My Jesus

He had no predecessor,
and He will have no successor.

He is the Lion,
and He is the Lamb.

He is God,
And He is Man.

He is the seven-way King:

He is the King of the Jews . . .
    that's a racial King.

He is the King of Israel . . .
    that's a national King.

He is the King of righteousness . . .
    that's a moral King.

He is the King of the ages . . .
    that's an eternal King.

He is the King of heaven . . .
    that's a universal King.

He is the King of glory . . .
    that's a celestial King.

He is the King of kings and the Lord of lords!

My Jesus is . . . *Everything!*

Before dawn,

in the inky blackness of night, the soldiers stood guard over Jesus' tomb. Knowing that to go to sleep on duty was an offense punishable by death, they remained alert. Suddenly, "there was a violent earthquake" (Matthew 28:2 NIV). Almost simultaneously, the predawn darkness was split by a light so brilliant it looked like a laser of lightning! The lightning took the shape of an angel who seemed to reach from heaven to earth, who walked over to the stone that blocked the tomb's entrance, flicked it away as if it were dust, and the gaping hole where the stone had been revealed that there was no one inside!

The tomb was empty.
Jesus had arisen from the dead.

Nothing could be more contrary

to our personal comfort or more challenging to our faith than death because it is the greatest storm we will ever face, whether it's our own death or that of a loved one.

But there is a greater miracle than physical healing! It's the miracle of the resurrection! God promises you and me that we will have His presence as we walk through the valley of the shadow of death or deep waters or fiery trials.

Has God increased the pressure in your life? Then praise Him, not for the pressure, but for His transforming power at work that will use it to produce His character in you until others can see Him. Paul described it this way:

> *"We have this treasure in jars of clay to show*
> *that this all-surpassing power is from God and*
> *not from us. We are hard pressed on every side,*
> *but not crushed; perplexed, but not in despair;*
> *persecuted, but not abandoned; struck down,*
> *but not destroyed. We always carry around in*
> *our body the death of Jesus, so that the life of*
> *Jesus may also be revealed in our body."*

2 CORINTHIANS 4:7–10 (NIV)

God the Father split history in two when

He flexed the divine, eternal muscle of His will and exerted His power on His Son's behalf! How He must have eagerly anticipated and rejoiced in the vindication and resurrection of His Son! His power was so mightily tremendous that Jesus was

Raised up from the dead!

Raised up without our sin!

Raised up to life!

Raised up through the walls of the tomb!

Raised up past the guards!

Raised up through all His invisible enemies!

Raised up to a position of authority over the entire
    universe!

Raised up to be seated at the right hand of God!

Jesus was raised up!

He's alive!

And nothing can ever be the same again!

Because Jesus found us

in our hopeless, helpless state and offered us His hand at the cross, we can be welcomed into heaven. If we accept His offer and put our hand of faith in His, He will walk with us hand in hand, not only through the remainder of our journey, but through the gates of heaven that will be opened wide for us.

After the long journey of life, we are going to look up and see heaven.

We're going to hear voices lifted in songs of praise. We're going to see the glory of God radiating from within, and we're going to long for home.

We will be as welcomed and accepted in heaven as He is, solely because of our relationship and identification with Him. Praise God! Jesus is the One, and the only One, Who makes heaven available to the sinner, not only through the cross, but also through His resurrection.

Heaven has been opened! It is finished! To receive salvation . . . forgiveness of sin . . . acceptance by God . . . eternal life . . .

You don't have to do more good works than
    bad works.
You don't have to go to church every time the
    door opens.
You don't even have to go to church.
You don't have to count beads.
You don't have to climb the stairs to some statue.
You don't have to lie on a bed of nails.
You don't have to be religious.
You don't even have to be good!

It is finished! Salvation is free! Sin is forgivable!
The price has been paid! Jesus paid it all!

Hallelujah!

Hallelujah!

Hallelujah!

Jesus—the only One—makes

God visible
And change possible
And happiness attainable
And resources ample
And suffering understandable
And sin forgivable
And heaven available!

My Jesus is . . . *Everything!*

Let the word of Christ dwell in you richly
as you teach and admonish one another with all wisdom,
and as you sing psalms, hymns and spiritual songs
with gratitude in your hearts to God.
And whatever you do, whether in word or deed,
do it all in the name of the Lord Jesus,
giving thanks to God the Father through him.

Colossians 3:16–17

Anne Graham Lotz

STEPS TO PEACE WITH GOD

1. RECOGNIZE GOD'S PLAN—PEACE AND LIFE

The message in this book stresses that
God loves you and wants you
to experience His peace and life.

The BIBLE says ... *For God so loved the world
that He gave His only begotten Son, that
whoever believes in Him should not perish
but have everlasting life.* John 3:16

2. REALIZE OUR PROBLEM—SEPARATION FROM GOD

People choose to disobey God and go
their own way. This results in separation
from God.

The BIBLE says ... *For all have sinned
and fall short of the glory of God.*
Romans 3:23

3. RESPOND TO GOD'S REMEDY—THE CROSS OF CHRIST

God sent His Son to bridge the gap. Christ
did this by paying the penalty of our sins
when He died on the cross and rose from
the grave.

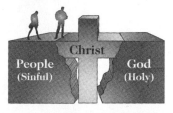

The BIBLE says ... *But God demonstrates
His own love toward us, in that while
we were still sinners, Christ died for us.*
Romans 5:8

4. RECEIVE GOD'S SON—LORD AND SAVIOR

You cross the bridge into God's family
when you ask Christ to come into your life.

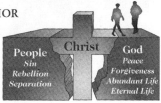

The BIBLE says ... *But as many as received
Him, to them He gave the right to become
children of God, to those who believe in
His name.* John 1:12

THE INVITATION IS TO:

REPENT (turn from your sins), ASK for God's forgiveness, and by faith RECEIVE
Jesus Christ into your heart and life and follow Him in obedience as your Lord
and Savior.

PRAYER OF COMMITMENT

"Dear Lord Jesus, I know that I am a sinner, and I ask for Your forgiveness. I believe
You died for my sins and rose from the dead. I turn from my sins and invite You to
come into my heart and life. I want to trust and follow You as my Lord and Savior.
In Your Name, amen."

If you are committing your life to Christ, please let us know!

Billy Graham Evangelistic Association
1 Billy Graham Parkway, Charlotte, NC 28201-0001
1-877-2GRAHAM (1-877-247-2426)
BillyGraham.org/Commitment